BYGONE SOUTHAMPTON

Endpapers: The High Street was one of Southampton's
main attractions. At one time it was claimed to be 'the
finest street of any town in England', and in 1796 it was
described as being ¾ of a mile long, well paved and lighted,
and terminating picturesquely at the quay.

Bygone Southampton

GEORGIAN AND VICTORIAN ENGRAVINGS AND PAINTINGS

Jan Stovold

Phillimore

1984

Published by
PHILLIMORE & CO. LTD.
Shopwyke Hall, Chichester, Sussex

ISBN 0 85033 553 1

Lithographic origination by
THOMAS CAMPONE
Southampton

Printed and bound in Great Britain by
OXFORD UNIVERSITY PRESS

LIST OF ILLUSTRATIONS

For Ashley and Oliver

ACKNOWLEDGEMENTS

I should like to thank all those who have helped in the preparation of this book. Special thanks must go to Professor Colin Platt, of Southampton University, who supervised my research into the spa period and read an earlier draft of this present book, making some helpful suggestions. Robert Douch, of the Department of Adult Education, has maintained a continued interest in my classes in Georgian and early Victorian Southampton, and given much encouragement.

Particular thanks are due to Geoffrey Hampson and his staff at the Special Collections, Southampton University Library, who introduced me to their collection of prints and gave permission for their reproduction. In addition, I would like to thank Sheila Thompson and the staff of the City Record Office, Southampton, for their invaluable assistance. Further thanks must go to the Southampton Art Gallery and Museums and the City Reference Library.

I acknowledge with gratitude permission to reproduce the following: City Record Office, nos. 15, 23, 55, 59, 94, 95, 96, 100, 106, 111, 114, 117, 118, 119; no. 30 (in City Record Office, courtesy of Mr. Duncan); no. 85 (in City Record Office, courtesy of Mr. Hawes); no. 120 (in City Record Office, courtesy of the British Associated Ports); Southampton Art Gallery, nos. 19, 38, 41, 49, 56, 91, 97; Southampton Museum, nos. 31, 32; Hampshire County Library, no. 34. All other plates are from the Cope Collection and reproduced by courtesy of Southampton University Library.

Introduction

TOWARDS THE MIDDLE of the 18th century, the port of Southampton was in a state of industrial and commercial decline. Rival coastal ports such as Poole and Weymouth had started to attract foreign trade away from Southampton.

The Corporation, only vaguely aware of the impoverishment that faced the town, suggested mediocre measures to recapture that trade—firstly, the abolition of petty customs on goods imported from Africa or America, and secondly, an extension to Watergate Quay, 'to admit larger ships to load or unload there . . . and also to make a provision for the more safe lying there of ships in bad weather'.[1]

Many contemporary observers described Southampton at this time as 'decayed' and 'neglected', attributing the overall crumbling appearance of the town to the failure of the port. Celia Fiennes observed, 'but now the trade has failed and the town almost forsooke and neglected', whilst Daniel Defoe thought the place was 'dying with age; the decay of the trade is the real decay of the town'.[2]

From the 1720s onwards the habit of drinking mineral waters and even of bathing in the sea had been increasing in popularity, and when 'persons of quality' discovered Southampton it was soon established as a fashionable spa. Notable people began to follow the example set by the Earl of Peterborough who, after a distinguished career in the army, retired to Bevois Mount, a rented house on the south coast. He later bought and enlarged his estate so that in time it stretched from Rockstone Lane and across the Avenue. There he entertained a variety of eminent visitors in the 'solemn-gloomy wilderness' of his garden perched high above the bay of the River Itchen. So entranced was he with this view that he would admit no visitors into his garden except when the tide was high, for only then did he believe was the view complete.

Probably the greatest boost to the spa's development came in 1750 in the person of Frederick, Prince of Wales. Whilst visiting the New Forest, he came to Southampton to bathe in the water which he promptly declared was 'salubrious and invigorating'. He also expressed a particular desire to be admitted to the town as an honorary burgess, and a delighted Corporation suggested that: 'His Royal Highness the Prince of Wales be presented with a Copy of his freedom of this Town in a Gold Box . . . of about twenty guineas value . . .'. The Corporation actually overspent: the gold box cost £35 11s. 6d.[3] However, it was money well spent, for Frederick's visits to the town soon set a fashion, despite the fact that the Prince himself died less than three months after his ceremonious acceptance of the Freedom. He caught a chill after playing tennis at Kew, and died of pleurisy in March 1751.

Fortunately for the town he had made his all-important visit just in time, for where royalty went, the nobility and gentry were soon to follow. Men of rank discovered that Southampton had become an exclusive retreat for the summer season where they could be assured of meeting others of good breeding. 'Most gentlemen of this town', explained a guide book, 'are men of fortune, independence, and generosity, who keep the happy medium between avarice and extravagance, meanness and profusion; men who do not debase their characters by an intimacy with the vulgar and their manners, nor proudly despise their equals...'.[4]

New patrons were quickly found in the late Prince's three younger sons, the Dukes of York, Cumberland and Gloucester, and it was their patronage in particular that was to become of the greatest importance. Their visits, of course, made excellent press reports:

> His Royal Highness the Duke of York arrived here on Monday last; and after having dined at Sir John Mordaunt's, at Bevis Mount, went to the assembly, which was opened by His Royal Highness and Lady Barker; minuets were danced till half past nine; after which His Royal Highness danced two or three country dances, drank tea, and withdrew about twelve. His Royal Highness still continues at Sir John Mordaunt's. We have many persons of distinction lately arrived and others daily coming in.[5]

By 1781 the Corporation was able to boast that it had more royal burgesses than any other town in England. And young royalty gladly took part in the elegant, provincial life. They attended balls and other social functions, supported important events, and encouraged the crowds wherever they went. The *Fox*, a frigate of 28 guns, was launched at Northam in September 1773,

> in the presence of a prodigious concourse of people, among whom were His Royal Highness the Duke of Gloucester, the Duke and Duchess of Bolton, the Duke of Richmond and various others of the nobility and gentry. There were above fifty gentlemen's carriages, and the ship went off remarkably well.[6]

The royals took rented houses in town. The report that the Duke and Duchess of Cumberland had taken the centre house in the Polygon, 'where, we hear, they intend to reside for two months', prompted another announcement that 'The town has filled so amazingly lately, that there are scarce any lodgings to be procured'.[7] Special requests were made, too, to the theatre, where the managers gratefully advertised this patronage:

> On Wednesday, (by command of the Duke and Duchess of Gloucester) the comedy *She Stoops to Conquer*, with the farce of the *Irish Widow*, was performed (with much applause) to a crowded audience.—So desirous were all orders of people of paying their respects to the Royal pair, that before six o'clock the house was as full as possible, and before their Royal Highnesses arrival, more than £20 had been turned away.[8]

In fact, anything that the royal family did made good newspaper copy. The Duke of Cumberland had apparently ordered his household to be paid their arrears of wages before he set out for the season in Southampton; another favourite, the Duke of Bolton, was appreciably reported as having distributed £300 amongst the Hampshire poor. And the Duke of Richmond commissioned a yacht to be built on the River Itchen, whilst the Duchess of Gloucester, 'with her usual benevolence', clothed the poor men and women of Lyndhurst.[9] In

August 1774 the Duke and Duchess of Cumberland travelled down the river in a concourse of barges 'with music, and colours flying' to view the shipping at Spithead. The spectacle of the spa was greatly enhanced by all this pageantry.

*　　*　　*　　*　　*

Southampton had a unique dual advantage to offer the summer visitor; mineral waters from a chalybeate spring, and sea-bathing facilities. Many doctors in the 18th century had taken to prescribing 'cold-bathing' as a cure for all sorts of illnesses, especially in cases where medicines alone had proved ineffectual. Semi-paralysis, chronic rheumatism and gout were all said to benefit admirably from the Baths, and even more so if bathing was employed in conjunction with 'douche and dry-pumping upon ailing parts', following a full course of at least five or six weeks. Dr. Granville, a well-known figure around spa towns, advocated a minimum amount of movement whilst in the water:

> . . . quiescent posture is in my opinion essential . . . to fatigue the body by exercise during the operation of bathing, are circumstances which greatly militate against its good results . . .[10]

In 1760 Dr. Hales, who believed in the use of sea-water as preventive medicine, proclaimed:

> 'Tis well known that Persons who bathe in the sea, and then put their clothes on their wet Bodies, are not subject to catch cold . . . These considerations led me to think, that it might probably be a good method to *wet the body with salt water,* and then to put on their clothes on their wet Bodies . . .

Four years later Dr. Hasgin reaffirmed that 'sea-water . . . covers the skin with a saltish crust, *which prevents all feverish infections',* whilst Southampton's own Dr. Speed, famed as a local historian, experimented with Southampton water and deduced that it was 'a *cold medicated* Bath'.[11]

With all this medical encouragement it is hardly surprising that the Georgian gentry, suffering from gout and other complaints, flocked to the coastal resorts. Enterprising individuals in Southampton lost no time in erecting bathing establishments. Early on, the most popular baths proved to be Martin's Baths on the West Quay, where a special feature was the false-bottomed pool which was raised and lowered by a windlass according to the state of the tide, and meant that men and women could bathe there at all times. Non-bathers could walk alongside and watch those who had taken the plunge, and in 1775 a hot bath was added to the complex. Bathing was segregated, but nevertheless ladies were decently attired in long green flannel gowns and socks, which could be either hired or bought from Mrs. Martin, the charge for the hire being two shillings, payable at the end of the course of bathing. Hair was tied back in leather pouches, whilst an 'Oyl-silk Fillet' preserved the fashionable forehead curl. A guide would carry into the water those who were 'Infirm or want courage', and it was customary to pay the guide one shilling at each visit, although Mrs. Martin took eightpence out of this.[12]

Mr. Seward was the proprietor of another bathing establishment on the West Quay, advertised as being 'compact and commodious for people of fashion'. Further along were those of Mr. Webb, later taken over by Mr. Goodman, which were apparently adapted for those who swam.[13] The Gloucester Baths were built on the beach near the Platform, and were at one time exceptionally popular, whilst near were bathing machines at the Cross House.

In addition to being a seaside resort, Southampton was also famed for its mineral spring waters. Spa waters, despite being a distinctly acquired taste, were ritually drunk, frequently in large quantities. Generally, a middle-sized rummer or tumbler was taken once in the morning and again in the afternoon, followed by gentle exercise to aid the water's action. The chief source of the local chalybeate water was in a spring kept constantly covered so as to enhance its properties—most especially its reputation for healing jaundice, scurvy, paralytic disorders and for preventing barrenness.[14] Spa Gardens, sometimes called the Cherry Gardens, were laid out around this spring. Here subscribers could drink the waters and promenade along the seashore. Three times a week a band of musicians entertained the customers from 7 until 9 p.m. The Gardens were also renowned for their botanic collections, which included an extensive array of exotic and unusual plants. A reading room was established in which a valuable collection of botanical publications could be consulted. Subscriptions to these gardens cost 15 shillings a year per person, or £1 10s. 0d. for a family ticket, and entitled the holder to walk in the garden and greenhouses, peruse the books in the library, and remove plants, flower seeds or bouquets to half the amount of the subscription. The proprietor also kept a nursery at Hill, where other exotic plants were for sale. Non-subscribers who wished to drink the waters were asked to pay twopence each at the well, but the poor were allowed a free glass before 8 o'clock in the morning.

*   *   *   *   *

The most popular amusement in a spa town was dancing. Until 1761 the *Royal George* in the High Street had been the social venue, but as the spa progressed it was realised that these rooms were too small and inconvenient. Mr. Martin consequently built a new room along the West Quay, where the obvious attraction was the superior view across the water. The gardens around the rooms stretched out to the seashore, and quickly became a favourite promenade spot. The bathing establishment next door also offered rare sights, as the ingenious Mr. Martin had built a walkway alongside so that visitors could watch the 'evolutions of the bathers'. Throughout the 1760s, the company continued to increase, so that by 1767 Mr. Martin had to add another room, hence the title 'the Long Rooms'. No expense was spared, valuable chandeliers and pier-glasses provided a luxurious setting. In the centre of the room played the band, whilst adjoining the main dancing room were tea, card and billiard rooms.

Traditionally, the season commenced on 5 June, the King's birthday, by which time the town would be full with seasonal visitors. The amusements continued until October. Balls were given regularly, in some years three times a week. Every

Tuesday night a dress ball was held, for which subscribers paid 10s. 6d. for the season, and non-subscribers 3s. 6d. a time. Thursday was the night for 'undress balls or Cotillons', and Saturdays were reserved for country dances. Apart from the entrance fee it was also customary for the dancers to pay a shilling apiece to the musicians. As the years progressed, the cost of dancing also rose. By 1781 the subscription had risen to one guinea, the individual dance remaining at 3s. 6d. In 1795, however, the price did drop to 10s. 6d. again, but it was expected that following a custom, gentleman who danced would be asked to pay an extra 2s. 0d.[15] The Master of the Ceremonies was in strict command at the Assembly Rooms. He was responsible for issuing a set of rules for the dances which demanded in 1768, for example, that the balls should begin at 7 p.m. and end precisely at 11 p.m. The Master of Ceremonies had merely to look at his watch and this was the signal for the company to break up immediately, even if in the middle of a dance.

Children were allowed to attend, but they had to pay the same entrance fee as the adults. Ladies and gentlemen who intended to dance were required to send their name to the Box appointed for that purpose, and ladies were not permitted to dance in an apron, mittens or black gloves. Except where rank entitled the dancers to precedence, lots were drawn for places in the country dances. The Master of Ceremonies settled all questions of rank, and called the time for tea-drinking. Tea, or a dish of chocolate, was available for sixpence, 'except ladies that dance, as it is customary for their partners to pay for them'. It was also felt necessary to include in the rules that gentlemen were not expected to place themselves before ladies and prevent them watching the dancers, or continue to sit on the benches when ladies wanted seats.[16] More rules were added over the years. In 1774 gentlemen were requested not to come to the Long Rooms with boots on, and to leave their swords at the door. Altogether, the insistence was on formal ceremony and good manners. Even before newcomers to the town could take part in these dances it was expected that the Master of Ceremonies would call upon them at their lodgings or hotel to inquire into their right to enter his exclusive circle. If in doubt he could politely but firmly refuse them admittance.

Every winter the inhabitants' social life was not forgotten, but the venue was changed. In 1785 the Winter Assemblies were established at the *Dolphin Inn* in the High Street, held fortnightly on Tuesdays. This season cost another 7s. 6d. Since the Master of Ceremonies held so important a post it is not surprising that the position was much coveted. A quarrel broke out in 1777 when it was rumoured in the *Hampshire Chronicle* that Mr. Dawson, the longstanding Master of Ceremonies, had been elected to that post at the Upper Rooms at Bath. In order to elect a new official a meeting of the gentlemen of the town was called, but Dawson sent an open letter to the newspaper claiming he had no intention of resigning his post at Southampton. However, his position was 'solicited by a native of this town', and when it transpired that Dawson intended holding both posts, this prompted angry protest from those subscribers who actually lived in Southampton, whilst many 'fashionable' visitors announced Dawson should not be displaced. Dawson's friends appeared to be the most influential and finally his rival, the local man, Andrew Goater Haynes, declared he would, to preserve the peace, relinquish his claim.[17]

The increasing friction between the town's year-round inhabitants and the 'strangers' to Southampton may have been one of the reasons behind the plan to build the Polygon. Certainly, the visitors to the Long Rooms included people engaged in trade, and so the assembly may not have been as aristocratic as some newcomers would have liked. Added to this were the dangers of going to the Long Rooms after dark, down narrow lanes that were impossible to negotiate except on foot or by sedan chair. Mr. Martin had been only too aware of this drawback, and had successfully appealed to the Corporation to alter the town walls by Beidles Gate. Nevertheless, Blue Anchor Lane could not be used by vehicles of any size.

Speculative investors were not slow to realise that another assembly room in an expanding town might promise good investment returns. An 'intended assemblage of elegant edifices' was therefore designed by an architect from Great Russell Street—Jacob Leroux. The plan was for a group of buildings to the north of the town on such an elevation as to command views across Southampton Water as far as Calshot Castle, of the New Forest, Southampton itself, several gentlemen's seats, and even, in the distance, the Isle of Wight. Originally, the Polygon was a twelve-sided concept with a gentleman's villa in the centre of each side. Each house was to be equipped with all necessary outhouses, have gardens of one acre and an allotment of land in front to graze cattle. The whole site would extend for 22 acres and be bordered by a gravel road. Fronting outwards, the houses would face the countryside and river whilst their back gardens converged towards a lake. This basin of water would also supply all the houses. A central meeting place, to include a tavern, assembly and card rooms, and hotel was also planned. The design was heralded as Southampton's answer to Bath's Royal Crescent and Tunbridge's Pantiles. Financial backing was to come from a local property speculator, Isaac Mallortie, and General John Carnac, a retired officer of the East India Company who lived in Cams Hall, near Fareham. With great ceremony, Viscount Palmerston and the Honourable Hans Stanley laid the first stone in August 1768.[18] The hotel was due to open for the summer season of 1773, yet as early as 1769 the proprietors announced they had engaged an eminent tavern-keeper from London to run the complex.[19] Madame Cornelys arrived in Southampton on 4 June 1773, hailed as the 'Empress of Taste'.

All augured well for the opening of the Polygon. On 5 July it was announced that the first assembly at the Great House was fixed for 29 July, one of the wings of the building had been fitted up for dinner, and the principal dancer of the London Opera House was ready to give lessons. But there were doubts. Only three of the houses had been completed (the first two were occupied by the developers themselves), and questions were asked whether the whole design would ever be finished, or the opening date of the tavern satisfied. Rumours began to circulate that the Polygon would not be ready for its grand opening night. Notices appeared in the newspaper refuting this, assuring the nobility and gentry that 'it will be opened with all convenient speed', and laying the blame for any delay at the door of the workmen.[20] Eventually, the first assembly was held a month late, on 23 August 1773, near the end of the season and with the Great House still not completely ready. Still, it seemed as if the Polygon's season, although late, might still be off to a flying start with royal visitors, regular assemblies and a grand masked ball. The newspaper accounts of 13 September 1773 include an announcement for the fourth assembly, that costumes for the masked ball could be obtained from Pritchard's Masquerade Warehouse, and that Mallortie had become bankrupt and his estates were to be sold—including the Polygon. It was the death knell of the great project. The masquerade ball was reported as being sparsely attended. During the evening a large flint stone was thrown in at one of the windows and narrowly missed the Duchess of Gloucester and 'as it was thrown with great violence, had it struck her, it would most probably have done her an essential injury'.[21] The people of Southampton did not all appreciate the attractions of the Polygon. No one could be found who would buy the lease on the hotel. Mrs. Cornelys returned to London after a slow 1774 season, and the balls continued without competition at Martin's Rooms. Mrs. Cornelys had taken a thirty-year lease on the hotel, yet stayed for only two. In later years, the guide books pointed out the Polygon to visitors as a mild attraction—the gravel road in particular became a favoured place for taking the air, or a drive by carriage. By 1796 three of the houses were finished and inhabited, besides the hotel which was by then converted into two more dwellings.

$$* \qquad * \qquad * \qquad * \qquad *$$

Card games, sporting meetings and concerts were all essential for the society visitors, so, too, was the theatre. A theatrical company began performing every year at the Guildhall, and the success of these plays prompted the building of Southampton's own playhouse. In 1765 the manager, George Farran, issued a notice on the *Proposals for Building a Theatre,* wherein he and his company suggested that £157 10s. 0d. be raised by subscription 'which sum shall be employed and expended under the direction of Geo Farran for building the most commodious manner'. The share of each subscription was 10 guineas, and this entitled the holder to a seat in either of the boxes on thirty nights (over three seasons) or for an additional shilling each time to two seats in the pit. Fifteen gentlemen accordingly subscribed—men such as Nathaniel St André of Belle Vue, Arthur Atherley, and Harrison the future banker.

The theatrical company was actually under the management of Samuel Johnson by the time the theatre was built. In March 1766 Johnson announced he had taken a lease of a house in a back street and he proposed fitting it up on the plan of the Bath theatre. That July they opened with a production of *Venice Preserv'd,* performed before the Duke of Gloucester, and continued the season with such favourite pieces as *The Way to keep Him, The Suspicious Husband,* and a masque, *Comus,* which was very popular. From November the company had a regular circuit playing for four months at Salisbury, then going to Chichester for two months, and Winchester for another two months. But from 1766 they took to returning annually to Southampton for the summer season, playing Mondays, Wednesdays and Thursdays.

In 1769 John Collins was taken as a partner into the management of the theatre, and he himself took over the running of the establishment in 1770, taking James Davies as a partner in 1771. Collins and Davies shared the responsibility of the theatre between them. Actors traditionally received payment from 'benefit' performances, although in 1774 Collins engaged his first salaried actor, Thomas Robson. The aim of such a provincial theatre was to exhibit most of the new pieces that had appeared in London theatres the previous winter, and one of the first big scoops was Dr. Goldsmith's *She Stoops to Conquer*. Performances were very varied. A farce would normally be combined with a tragedy, and a hornpipe danced between the two. Criticisms were levelled at the length of the evenings' entertainments when in 1777 an anonymous complaint appeared in the local newspaper suggesting that 'a five act play and a farce or opera of two acts, with the addition of a song, or dance between the acts affords sufficient entertainment for one night'.[22]

By the end of the 18th century it was evident that the playhouse was too small. It was reported that some of the fashionable people were refusing to patronise the theatre because of its ruinous condition which was 'deplorable'. The lease on this site was due to run out in September 1803, so before that date Collins bought St John's Hospital in French Street nearly opposite the former theatre. The new playhouse was larger, and the company could now take over £100 per night. Benefit nights generally raised £60 to £70 for a favourite performer. The year 1801 had probably seen the theatre's proudest moment when Mrs. Siddons visited Southampton and gave three or four performances to a delighted audience. She was then 46, eleven years off retirement. She made a return visit in 1809, and lived in a spacious house in Portland Terrace.

*   *   *   *   *

As the spa waned in the first decade of the 19th century, new pastimes attracted leisured visitors, and the pleasure of horse-racing and yachting gave new life to the town. The Long Rooms were, by the 1820s, decidedly outmoded, if not unsafe, and a subscription company raised the necessary capital to build a new assembly room on the site of the spa gardens. Opened in 1830 and simply labelled the New Rooms, they attracted new patrons in the Southampton and New Forest Archery Club who liked to shoot in the pleasant gardens overlooking the water. In October 1830 these rooms were renamed the Royal Victoria Rooms, in honour of the Princess who had paid them a visit. Princess Victoria was again in Southampton on 8 July 1833 in order to formally open the Royal Pier. In 1803 Harbour Commissioners had taken over from the Corporation the management of the port, and after improving access to the quays by dismantling many waterside buildings, they began the construction of a new pier for the steam packets now in operation between Southampton and France, the Channel Islands, and the Isle of Wight.

Since the end of the Napoleonic Wars with France, passenger traffic had greatly increased, and the Southampton–Havre de Grace route was firmly established, whilst in 1819 passenger traffic to the Isle of Wight was said to be 'without precedent'.

Southampton's modern age, the return from elegance to commerce, had actually begun, for the speed of the new steam packets revolutionised sea crossings. Steamer excursions were ever popular, and for five shillings a visitor could enjoy a pleasure trip to Portsmouth and back. In 1831 the passage to Havre cost ten shillings, and Southampton was rapidly becoming the gateway to the Continent. With the incorporation of the Southampton Dock Company in 1836, and the completion of the Outer Dock in 1842, the town embarked upon a new and fruitful course: the Peninsular and Oriental Company's Far Eastern Service began in the 1840s, the Royal Mail Steam Packet Company's West Indian service was established in 1842, and the South-Western Company's cross-Channel services were started in 1845. The 1850s saw the beginnings of the Union Steamship Company's (forerunner of the Union-Castle line) service to South Africa, and the ships of the Hamburg-American line commenced calling en route from Germany to New York, soon followed by Norddeutscher Lloyd. With the transfer of American Line's New York service from Liverpool to Southampton in 1893, the town was well and truly established as a passenger port.

Work on a railway line from Southampton to London had also commenced early in 1835, and the first section of the line was opened on 21 May 1838. The completion of this line actually meant increased numbers of visitors to the town, as well as facilitating commercial undertakings, and later guide books took trouble to point out that 'the quiet, retired, and genteel character of the town as a watering-place' had not been destroyed. Rather, the construction of the docks and railways concentrated the wheels of commerce in one spot, 'the lower portion of the town', thus ensuring that the upper environs were 'rendered so quiet and comparatively sequestered, as to be far more suitable for genteel residences'.[23]

Throughout the last half of the 19th century Southampton continued to attract visitors. Gone were the former days of spa elegance, but the town perservered as a commercial resort, offering 'excellent hostelries' in the *South-Western*, Radley's the *Royal* and the *Dolphin* hotels. Visitors continued to find Southampton an attractive place to stay for 'the beauty of the surrounding country—the deep interest of its antiquities and historical associations—its convenience as a centre for land or water excursions—as well as for its safety and importance as a commercial port'.[24]

NOTES

1. *Corporation Journals,* 25 October 1754 and 8 May 1761.
2. C. Morris (ed.), *The Journeys of Celia Fiennes,* p.54; Cresset Press 1949.
   G.D.H. Cole (ed.) *A Tour through England and Wales: Daniel Defoe,* 1:141. Dent Everyman edition 1928.
3. *Corporation Journals,* 14 December 1750 and 21 June 1751.
4. *Baker's Guide to Southampton,* 1775, p.10.
5. *Salisbury Journal,* 27 June 1763.
6. *Hampshire Chronicle,* 6 September 1773.
7. Ibid., 15 August 1774.
8. Ibid., 6 September 1773.
9. Ibid., 29 January 1776, 19 May 1783, 5 September 1774.
10. For this and other doctors' reports see W. Addison, *English Spas* (London, 1951).
11. *Linden's Guide to Southampton,* 1768, pp. 27-9; *Baker's Guide to Southampton,* 1787: Treatise on the remarkable effects of seawater . . .
12. Quoted in R. Douch, *Visitors' Descriptions Southampton 1540-1956,* pp. 16-18.
13. *Cunningham's Guide to Southampton,* 1796, p.91.
14. Ibid, p.95.
15. *Baker's Guide to Southampton,* 1795, p.68.
16. *Linden's Guide to Southampton,* 1768, Rules for the Balls.
17. *Hampshire Chronicle,* 3 and 24 November, 1, 15 and 22 December 1777, 11 and 18 May 1778.
18. *Salisbury Journal,* 15 August 1768.
19. Ibid., 25 December 1769; *Hampshire Chronicle,* 24 May 1773.
20. *Hampshire Chronicle,* 2 August 1773.
21. Ibid., 20 September 1773.
22. Ibid., 6 October 1777.
23. P. Brannon, *The Picture of Southampton,* 1850, p.10.
24. Ibid., p.9.

The Plates

Days of Elegance and Commerce

The Setting

1. A view of the High Street looking north. 'Many of the shops rival in elegance those of the metropolis', suggested one guide book, whilst another of 1805 proudly boasted: '...the shopkeepers are equally strenuous to excel in the elegance of their shops and display of their goods. Strangers in general are exceedingly struck at the size and the very superior appearance of the shops in this town, nor are they less so on viewing the abundant stocks of goods with which they are stocked...'.

2.   View of the High Street: the Pavement Commissioners undertook to light the town, but it was not until 1782, after the completion of the paving project, that 150 lamps were placed along the main streets and in some of the back streets.

3.   Following an Act of Parliament in 1770, Pavement Commissioners were appointed to pave the main streets, paint street names and numbers, and, most importantly, remove obstacles and nuisances from the streets. All these things had a beneficial effect on the general appearance of Southampton. This view shows the High Street and Bar.

4.   This view shows the High Street. Wars with Fra[nce]
altered the character of life in the town for a time. [In]
1795 one visitor exclaimed 'we never saw a place t[hat]
had such a military appearance as Southampton' .
Earl Moira had assembled a large army in and aroun[d]
the town; six regiments had just set sail, 'but *where*
they did not know' , and nine regiments were still
encamped on Nursling Common. Fever was a grave
problem. In 1795 one regiment had just arrived fro[m]
Jersey 'where they had buried 250 men of a fever'

Drawn by W. Carpenter.

*Southampton Audit House & Market,
as it appeared on the night of the 25th of January 1842.
on the occasion of the Christening of the Prince of Wales.*

5. The Audit House and market, as it appeared on the occasion of the Christening of the Prince of Wales. In April 1771 the Corporation resolved to build a new Audit House 'for the better accommodation of the Body in their corporate concerns'. At the same time, it was agreed it would be more convenient to concentrate all the markets in one area, under shelter, and thereby improve the High Street 'both as to beauty and convenience'. The architect of this new, multi-purpose building was Crunden of Piccadilly, and his design provided for market space on the ground floor with the Corporation's offices above.

6. All Saints' Church, built in 1792-5 and designed by William Revesley. This popular church was famous for its vast unsupported internal roof span and its stuccoed classical temple appearance. Jane Austen attended this church, and her niece, born in April 1807, was christened here.

7. Along the front of Holy Rood Church ran a colonnade, known as the 'Proclamation Porch', since it was from here that public notices were proclaimed and the poll taken at elections.

8. St Lawrence Church, Southampton was described by Englefield as 'small, and almost choked up with houses erected around it'. He also believed that the church 'does not contain a single object either of beauty or antiquity'.

9.   This view shows St Michael's Church; fish markets were held in an adjoining building until 1773.

10. St Mary's, Southampton's mother church, stood outside the walls in the parish inhabited chiefly by the poorer labouring classes.

11. St Michael's Church and Square.

12. The Free Grammar School in Bugle Street had been 'very much out of repair' at the beginning of the spa period, but when the Reverend Mant was appointed headmaster in 1771 he made a number of improvements and the school was enlarged. The school rapidly grew into 'one of the most genteel and flourishing seminaries of learning in the country'.
13. Stray animals and unattended carriages were impounded in Above Bar at the *Pound Tree*. Aslatt and Son were famous coach-builders, and even as late as 1848 the manufacture of coaches was said to be the town's principal industry.

14. Prospect Place and Moira Place—two important areas of housing development situated a little to the north of Above Bar Street, yet still close enough to the central spa amenities. Sedan chairs, with strictly regulated rates for hire, were available for travel around the town. From any part of the town within the gates to any part without, the cost was ninepence.

15. Developers catered for the new demand for houses in the town by building fashionable squares and crescents, with the accent upon elegant, stuccoed designs in a healthy setting of 'airiness'.

6. During the spa period the town began to spread beyond its medieval bounds, and in particular, Above Bar Street was developed. Here, many new elegant houses were built for the leisured classes, and new hotels and coaching inns thrived. Coaches ran daily to London from a number of coaching inns in both Above Bar Street and the High Street, and several times a week to other resorts and towns.

17. Simnel Street: 1891. Housing within the intra-mural parishes was cramped and confined.
A multiplicity of courts, back-streets and alleyways were dominated by overhanging, old houses.

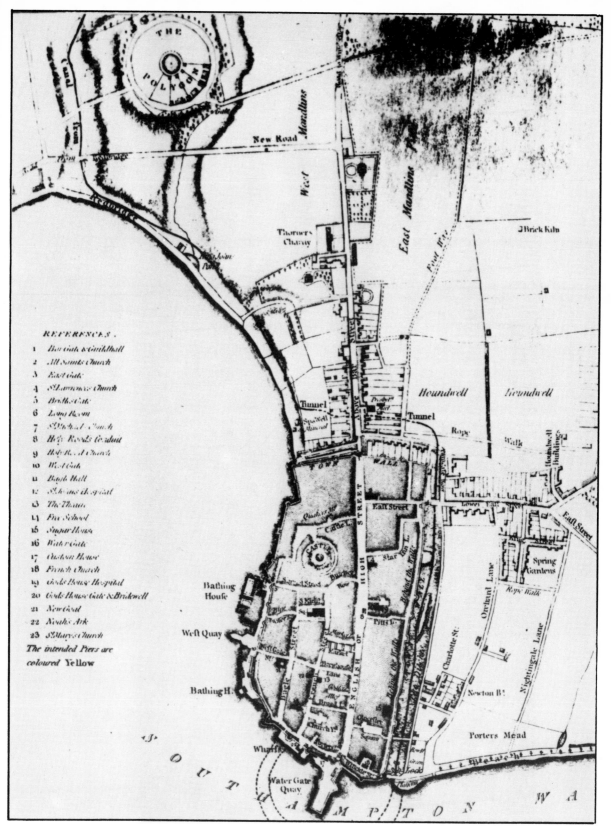

Map 1. Map of Southampton in 1791, by T. Milne.

The Amusements

(opposite page) Blue Anchor Lane, 1890. Visitors to the Long Rooms on the West Quay negotiated this lane, and
many complaints were received of the dangers of walking down such dark, narrow alleys, dressed for a ball, where pit-
falls were many and attacks by 'the mob' too frequent.

(below) 'A view of Southampton from near the Baths' by Samuel Austin (1796-1834).

20. The Town Walls, West Quay: in 1761 an assembly room was built on the quay, described as 'very elegant . . . handsomely Lighted up with five Glass Chandeliers'.

21. Men at work on the Arcade.

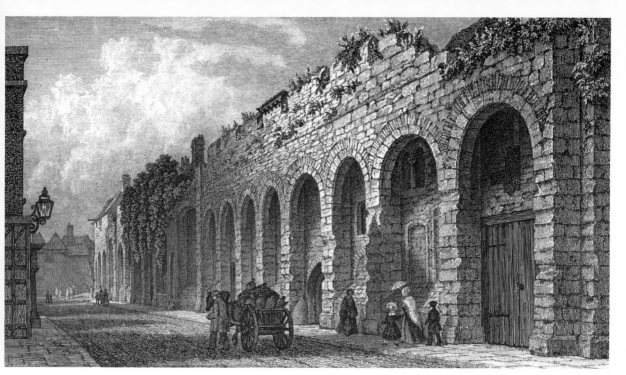

22. As early as 1756 Jonas Hanway wrote 'In this reign of SALTWATER, great numbers of people of distinction prefer SOUTHAMPTON for bathing . . .' (although he himself preferred the bathing-houses at Portsmouth). The most popular baths proved to be those adjacent to the Long Rooms, erected under the shore at West Quay. Spa visitors undertook a course of bathing, often following medical advice.

23. The New or Gloucester Baths and Promenade Rooms were built in 1829 along the Beach. The building was said to be of 'a very chaste design'.

24. The New Baths on the Beach. The New Baths were described as 'a most sumptuous and magnificent establishment, combining the *utile et dulce* of of bathing in a remarkable degree. Under the roof of this building are warm and cold, shower and vapour baths, with sulphur and other varieties of medicated baths. There are also plunging baths for ladies and gentlemen. The bathing rooms are fitted up with much taste and elegance, and attached to them is a subscription reading and news room, which is open to those who are waiting to take a bath.'

25. The new *Theatre Royal*, erected on the site of St John's Hospital in French Street, was said by Collins, the owner, to have cost him £3,000 in all. Designed by the architect Slater, the guide books claimed this playhouse was one of the best planned and most elegant in the country. However, Jane Austen had this to say: 'Martha ought to see the inside of the theatre before she leaves Southampton but I think she will hardly wish to take a second view . . .'.

26. The Royal Southern Yacht Club, formed in 1844, had its club house near the pier gates. Designed by Hack in an Italian style, this building was patronised by the nobility, in particular, whilst the rival Southampton Yacht Club was composed of the tradesmen of the town. Regattas of both clubs took place in July and August, and in addition several rowing and sailing matches were held at West Quay.

27. The Polygon houses had excellent views of the sea and town. The hotel had 50 bedchambers. Shops such as jewellers and peruke-makers (wig makers), were also within the complex.

28. For a short time before his death in 1809, the Marquis of Landsdowne lived in a Gothic-style castle. The castle site was put up for sale in 1816, but there was no buyer; it was demolished two years later. In 1823-4 the Zion Chapel was erected on the site.

29. Regatta Day. Spectators viewed the races from the pier, quays and platform whilst the yachtsmen competed for cups and money-prizes.

30. The Castle dominated the landscape. In 1810 one visitor gave this description: 'The Tower and upper part of the Building have a very fine appearance as you view it from Itchen Ferry and other places without the Town, but when you approach near, the *tout-ensemble* has a poor appearance . . . it is situated within the worst part of the Town, very confined and surrounded with mean little hovels occupied by the lowest description of poor people'.

31. Southampton Races on the Common, by T. G. Hart: horse-racing provided annual entertainment on the Common where the fashionable paraded.

2. The *Red Rover* coach, by Charles Hunt, 1837: by 1798 Southampton had become an important coaching centre with nearly 200 inward and outward coach movements each week. After 1800 Rogers, operating from the *Coach and Horses*, Above Bar, became the principal local coach operator. When he died in 1828 his business was taken over by William Caiger and Henry Wells.

33. High Street, 1858: the *Dolphin Inn*, in addition to being a coaching inn and the venue for the winter assemblies, also contained genteel shops and a subscription coffee-room called Brimyard's. There gentlemen could read the *Morning Post, Morning Herald, Morning Chronicle, Lloyd's Evening Post,* the *Gazette* and local newspapers such as the *Salisbury Herald* and *Hampshire Chronicle*. London papers would arrive only one day late.

34. In Carlton Place a riding-school was built, designed by Hinves, and described as 'very lofty and extensive, with an open timber roof'. It was said to have cost nearly £3,000.

35. The Royal Victoria Spa and Assembly Rooms, *c*. 1848: the Rooms in Portland Place became the new venue for visitors in the 19th century: 'On entering from Portland Street', explained Brannon, 'there is a lobby with ante-rooms, and from these a handsome staircase conducts to the main building, which consists of a great Ball-room 90 feet long, with a handsome card-room adjoining—a wide balcony is carried along the river-fronts of both. Below are rooms of equal extent, for refreshment during balls, and for meetings'.

. Royal Victoria Archery Grounds and Assembly Rooms: the Victoria Spa was situated in the grounds of the Victoria
·oms. Spa waters were still in use for some considerable time, and were even bottled and exported to the East and West
·dies and elsewhere.

The Antiquities

37. The Bargate, 1802: Southampton's visitors were encouraged by numerous guide books published from 1768 onwards, to take note of the town's historical attractions. In particular, the Bargate was singled out as 'a truly beautiful specimen of medieval military architecture' and 'a fine remain of antiquity'.

38. Bargate, Southampton, by Pryce Carter Edwards.
39. In 1765 a passage was cut for pedestrians through the east arch of the Bargate, and a few years later another was made through the west passage. Chairmen and handcarts continued to use the main carriageway.

40. The Bargate provided the visitor with a striking entry into Southampton from the London road. On the n
front were portrayed two gigantic figures, one on each side of the gateway, representing the warrior Ascupart
Sir Bevois of Southampton.

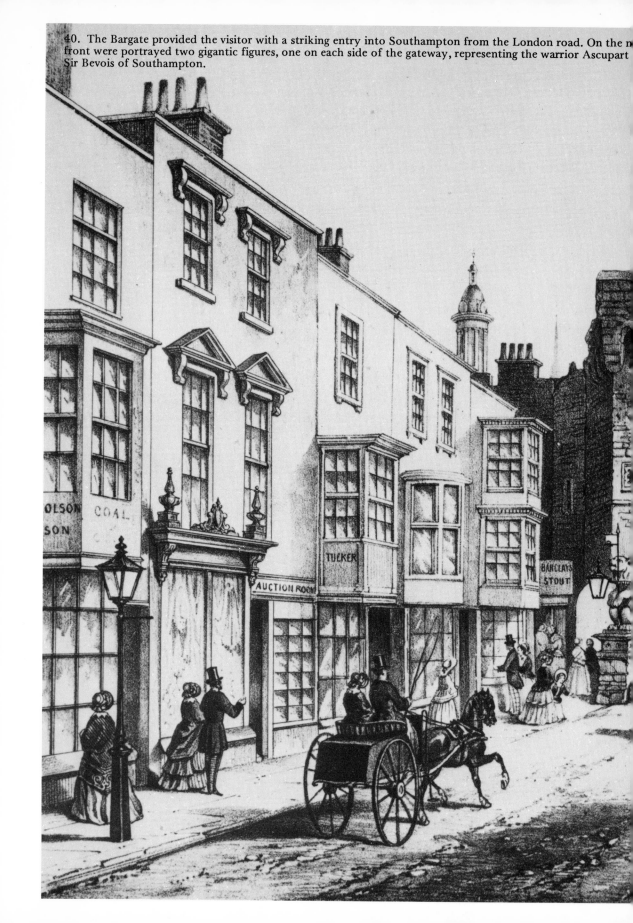

41. (*opposite page*) High Street and Bargate, Southampton, by R. Cook (1784-1857).

42. (*above*) The Bargate, 1814: the two lions were presented by William Lee, Esq., in 1774, on his being made a burgess, to replace two others which were then 'decayed'. They were cast in lead. In 1809 the Marquis of Lansdowne presented a statue of George III, wearing the imperial dress of the Emperor Hadrian, to the town, and it was placed on the south side of the Bargate.

43. In April 1775 the Pavement Commissioners sold the East Gate to William Daman, a local speculator, for £29. The gate was to be taken down within six weeks 'for the publick conveniency'. The Pavement Commissioners had, the previous month, paid the Corporation £16 for their interest in the gate, when leave was sought to demolish it. The Commissioners also subsequently gained permission to take down the wall on the south side of the bridge without East Gate, in order to widen the bridge. Daman had recently purchased the adjoining land, too, and he was given liberty to 'carry his buildings to the extreme boundary of the site of the said wall so to be taken down'.

Above the South or God's House Gate was the town gaol. In 1707 the Bridewell had been established there, and during 1770s the town's prisons were concentrated at God's House. The debtor's gaol remained at the Bargate, but was removed 786. God's House Tower continued as a prison until 1855 when it was 'left neglected' as a corn store. In 1874 it was ed by the Harbour Board.

45. Following the first Southampton Harbour Act it was announced that the Water Gate was very narrow and 'incommodious for trade', and that it would be to the benefit of the public if it was taken down and removed. Accordingly, in 1803 the Water Gate was advertised for auction at the *Globe Inn*. It was sold to J. Slater for £70.

46. The West Gate led to the fashionable spa venues along the West Quay.

47. The Watergate, 1814.

48. West Gate, 1807: through the arch can be seen the sign of the *Man in the Moon*, the base from which John Fisher 'equipped with all conveniences' undertook dipping in the salt water. Southampton water was said to hold the antidote for those bitten by mad dogs. In 1761 Fisher's colleague, Saul Jones, died 'mad' following a bite from a gentleman's dog: 'He was often desired to be dipped himself, but neglected it till it was too late'.

49. Tower, near York Buildings, Southampton, by Edward Dayes (1763–1804).

50. Visitors enjoyed a walk along the town's old fortifications. The total circuit of the walls was said by Englefield to be 2,200 yards or 1¼ miles.

51. The tide washed this section of the walls. Gradually, wharfs and timber-yards were built out into the water in front of the towers.

Promenades and Excursions

52. (*opposite page*) St Edward's Tower, otherwise known as Arundel Tower.

53. (*opposite page*) The North West Walls of Southampton: the Forty Steps were built in 1835. The terrace above was said to be much liked by Turner 'on account of the beauty of the sunsets seen from it'.

54. (*below*) In front of the Platform were some celebrated oyster beds, which at one time produced oysters worth £8,000 a year.

55. (*opposite, above*) A favourite waterside promenade ground overhung with rows of elms, the Platform also held a saluting battery of brass guns. Visitors would gather here, often as a prelude to walking along the Beach— a tree-lined walk made in 1769 on the old causeway from the Platform to Cross House. In June 1789 George III, with the Queen and two of their daughters, drove along the Beach, and were impressed by 'the grandeur of the view, enriched by a high tide'.

56. (*opposite, below*) Southampton: mouth of the old canal, by William Shayer, 1812: in the 1790s a scheme was prepared to construct a canal between Southampton and Salisbury. However, the project failed, and in 1808 the Canal Committee held its last meeting. The water became stagnant and in 1820 complaints were made of the stench under the gaol at God's House Tower which was 'injurious to prisoners'.

57. (*above*) A promenade in front of God's House Gate.

58. (*below*) Southampton from the water: a view of the Platform, 1840.

59. The walk towards Itchen Ferry was ever-popular. '. . . there is a double row of Trees all the way', one promenader described it, 'and on the right you look direct upon the Southampton Water which is an arm of the Sea, about 9 miles in length and nearly three, in breadth, the Country on each side is finely wooded and very Picturesque. At the Ferry are Machines for Bathing, which is pretty good. A Fine Sailing Vessel belonging to the Margravine of Anspach, is generally stationed here'.

60. The *Royal Oak* welcomed visitors who had made the ferry excursion across the Itchen. Nearby was a shipbuilder's yard.

61. The Cross House provided shelter for passengers waiting for the boat across the Itchen.

62. In 1808 Jane Austen took her nephews on the Itchen Ferry. (Drawing of 1795)

63. A view of Southampton from Pear Tree Green, 1772.

64. Northam Bridge, 1779, by Younge.

65. Northam Bridge and Farm.

66. In 1796 the Northam Bridge Company was set up to build a wooden bridge across the Itchen, and improve the approach roads. The bridge was opened in 1799. It was designed by Moneypenny, and erected upon four piles. The view from the bridge was spectacular—the sweep of the river at high tide, the site of Roman Clausentum on the east bank, and on the west the shipyards at Northam.

67. Waterside activities along the pier attracted the interests of many promenaders.

68. Opening ceremony of the Cobden Bridge, 1883. The National Liberal Land Company spent £11,500 on a 'noble iron bridge' to connect the Bitterne Park Estate with the town centre. On 27 June 1883 'Cobden Free Bridge' was officially handed over to the Mayor 'for the free use of the inhabitants forever'. In contrast, a toll was charged at Northam Bridge until 1929.

69.   Southampton from Pear Tree Green: crossing to the opposite bank of the water, visitors were rewarded with
excellent view of both the Itchen and Southampton Rivers, often full of sailing vessels. Cobbett wrote of Ridgeway
them that delight in water scenes, this is the prettiest place that ever I saw in my life'.

70. 'Paying a sloop's bottom', 1783.

71. A view of Southampton from the Round Hill.

72. The ruins of Netley Abbey and Netley beach, on the eastern bank of Southampton Water, were described by guide books as 'highly beautiful'.

73. 'For water excursions', claimed a guide book, 'Southampton possesses great attractions. The calmness of its land-encircled river induces the most timid female to venture herself upon it . . .'.

74. In 1745 the Corporation undertook the planting of trees along the main road to London across the Common. This avenue formed a renowned entrance to the town.

75. A 'new road' was made from Above Bar through the Marlands to the shore in 1791, and soon became a fashionable promenade rivalling in popularity the Beach Walk of the Platform to Cross House. The New Road later became Commercial Road.

76. One visitor described the Avenue on the Common in 1798: 'The idea of an avenue as a connecting thread between a town and a country, is a good one. We observe, however, that the beauty of this avenue is much greater as we approach Southampton, than as we leave it. As we leave it, the avenue ends abruptly in a naked country; but as we turned round, and viewed it in retrospect, it united with the woody scene around it, which had a good effect . . .'.

77. Regent's Park, near Southampton: carriages and horses were available for hire if required. One advertisement proclaimed: 'Persons who are fond of moving about at the rate of eight miles an hour may do so by engaging a landau and a pair of spirited horses; while others, who study economy more, and are contented to ride soberly to their journey's end, will be quite at home in a fly, drawn by a single horse'.

78. This view shows Milbrook, one of several large country estates built around Southampton. Visitors were actively encouraged by the guide books to go for a drive out of these country houses and view the splendid settings.

79. Bitterne from Bevois Mount.

80. The Earl of Peterborough was so entranced with this view from his gardens at Bevois Mount, that he only liked visitors to walk in his garden when the tide was high, for then the view was complete.

81. Shirley House.

82. The walk west, along the Blechynden shore.

83. 'The town runs out like a peninsula on the left, and, with its old walls and towers, makes a picturesque appearance'.

84. Southampton, from Hill Shore.

85. 'Lunar Rainbow seen at Milbrook, near Southampton, at 10 o'clock at night October 1810.'

86. In 1834 application was made to Parliament for a bill enabling a company to erect a bridge over the Itchen from Cross House to Itchen Ferry village. It was felt, however, that such a bridge would prove an obstacle to the building of ships of war at Northam. Finally, permission was obtained for a floating bridge which would take both foot passengers and carriages. In the autumn of 1836 it was opened.

87. The Priory of St Dionisius.

88. The Priory of St Dionisius. Between 1778 and 1812 the site of the priory was owned by General Stibbert, who erected new farm buildings on the land. The west end of the priory church with a small section of the south wall was still standing, and the ruins became a favoured picnic spot.

9. The average time for crossing via the floating bridge was four minutes—a great improvement on the old ferry which sometimes took a quarter of an hour or more, depending on the state of the tide and the wind. Passengers taking the bridge shortened a journey to Gosport or Portsmouth by three miles.

90. (*left*) The floating bridge was a large flat-bottomed vessel which plied between two chains stretched parallel from one bank to the other. There was said to be ample standing for several vehicles or horses, and apartments for passengers who could, if they wished, pay an extra halfpenny for 'exclusiveness'.

91. Southampton, 1861, by Philip Brannon.

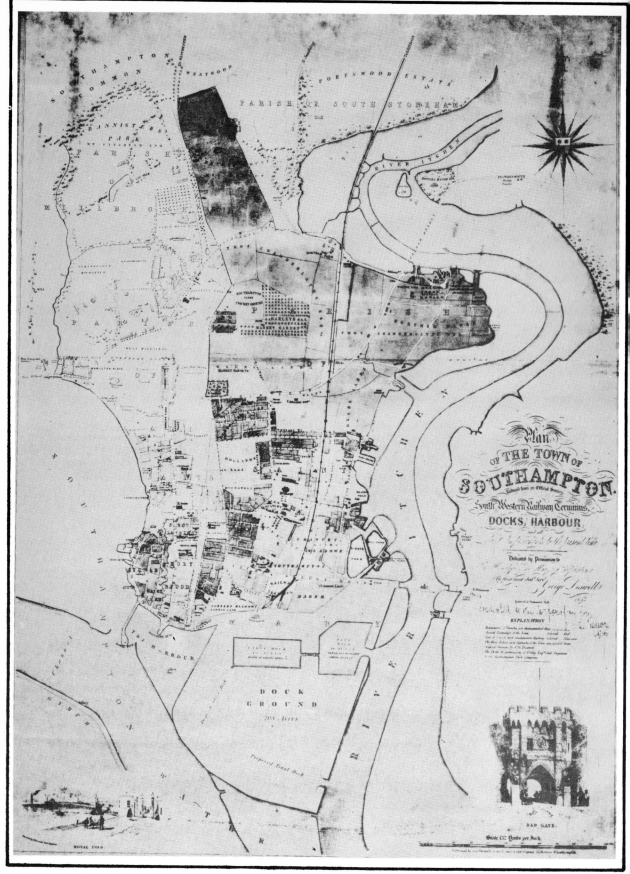

Map 2. Map of Southampton in 1842: official railway and docks survey.

Docks and Railways

92. On 21 May 1838 the line between London and Woking Common was opened. It was extended to Basingstoke by June 1839, when the section between Southampton and Winchester was also opened.

Drawn by W.Carpenter   *Engraved by J.Newman*

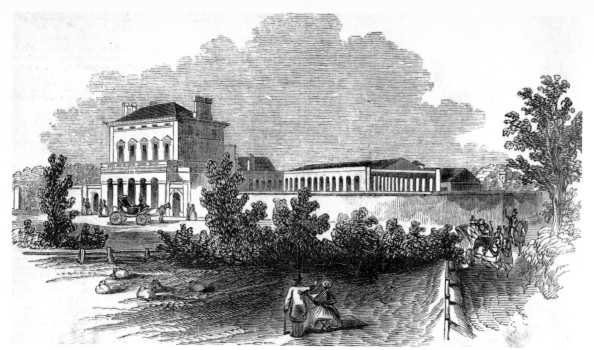

93. The plan for a railway from Southampton to London originated in 1825, and met with considerable encouragement at the time. However, it was not until 1832–4 that the bill was brought before Parliament, receiving the royal assent in July 1834. Early in 1835 work commenced. The original choice of engineer was Francis Giles, but when his competence was questioned he was replaced by Joseph Locke, who was recognised as one of the most distinguished civil engineers in the country.

94. The railway terminus was situated near the Platform and was of a 'very bold design in the Italian style', by the architect, Sir William Tite. The line throughout, between London and Southampton, was finally opened on 11 May 1840, and the terminus completed in time. Omnibuses ran a free service between the terminus and the *Star Hotel*, and for a while so great was the confusion and excitement at the terminus that police had to be called in.

95. Holy Trinity Church, Kingsland. Sheep and cattle grazed on the grassland in front of the station.
96. In 1840 the trains carried only first-class passengers and their servants (who had to be in livery).

97. A view of Southampton West Station *c.*1875-1880. Artist unknown.

98. Millbrook Shore: a stroll along the beach was enhanced by a glimpse of a steam-engine, where the line passed close to the shore.

99. Before the new pier was built, passengers from vessels were not only landed ashore in small boats, but at low spring tides were obliged to walk along a gravelled hard 'which as the tide had recently left it, was generally swampy'.

100. The Royal Pier, opened in 1833, was designed by the civil engineer, John D. Doswell. A broad gravelled carriageway was flanked throughout its length by a footpath on each side, which soon became another favourite promenading spot.

101. Southampton Pier, c. 1830. The pier extended nearly 300 yards from the quay: 'The prospects from it are of unequalled beauty, commanding a panoramic view of the opposite sylvan shore, the mouth of the Itchen and the Isle of Wight in the distance. At high water the scene is highly animated'.

London, Published by Hollyer.

Southampton

102. The Royal Pier: the Pier entrance was through handsome iron gates. Visitors were in the habit of promena along the pier 'where the sea breezes may be safely inhaled by those who are too timid to venture on the water in boats'.

103. The Gas Column, Quays and Victoria Pier: the columns for the street gas-lamps had been presented to the town by W. Chamberlayne, Esq., of Weston Grove, a Liberal M.P.: 'To commemorate this act of munificence a large cast-iron column, surmounted by an urn, has been erected on the Quay by public subscription. It is very useful as a sea-mark'.

104. Promenaders could pay an annual or half-annual subscription to walk along the pier. In the middle of the head of the pier was a refreshment room.

105. Many of the gentlemen and nobility of the neighbourhood kept yachts at Southampton. Other boats could be hired 'at all hours of the day, on reasonable terms' and 'attended by civil and skilful men'.

106. At the bottom of the High Street, four good inns were situated near the quay: the *Royal George*, the *Vine*, the *Castle* and the *Sun*. Several offices also provided information on the cross-Channel packets and other vessels.

107.   Southampton Pier with the Isle of Wight steamboat.

108. The *Royal Hotel*.

109. Bernard Street: Next to the *Clarendon Family Hotel,* the hot and cold showers and vapour baths.

110. A train approaching the Terminus, ships in the docks, and steam-packets at the Pier; Southampton's new commercial age.

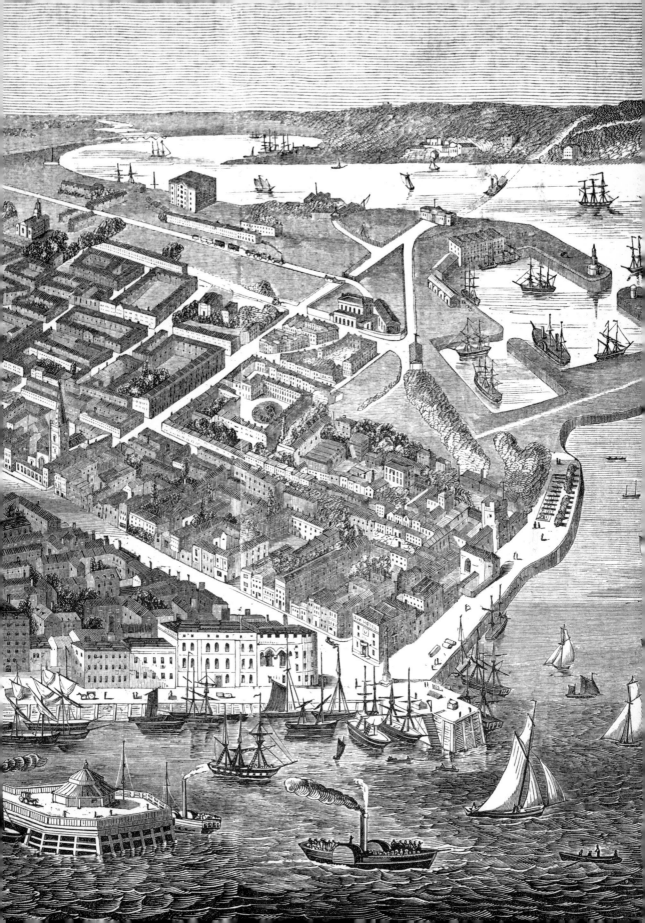

The Custom House, Southampton.

Eng.d by Harris Bro.s Lon

111. The old Custom House had been on the quay, adjoining the *Castle Inn*, but a new building was opened in 1846, facing the road from the Terminus, and of 'a simple yet very effective design'.

112. Offices of the P. & O. Company and entrance to the Docks, Canute Road. The Peninsular and Oriental Steam Packet Company secured the important government contract for the Peninsular, Mediterranean and Indian mails, and operated from Southampton.

113. Following the ceremonious laying of the first stone of the new docks on 26 October 1838, the Tidal Dock was opened in 1842. It measured 150 feet in width, and boasted 18 feet depth of water 'at the lowest spring tides'.

114. The Tidal Docks with the *Dauntless, Moulton, Nashville* and the *Tuscarora.*

115. The Peninsular and Oriental Steam Packet Company had in the 1850s 'nearly thirty steamships, many of them of the largest size, and all splendidly built and fitted-up'; the Royal West India Mail owned 15, and the New South-Western had about ten packets. The Isle of Wight Royal Mail Packet Company, and coastal steamers, also used the port.

116. An anonymous observer gave his impressions of Southampton in 1849: 'The town has assumed the busy look a great commercial city, and one is astonished at the rapid change, that is hourly taking place in this, till the last few years, little better than a local harbour . . .'.

117. The *Boscawen* training ship at Southampton, showing the Town Quay and the Gas Column.

118. (*opposite, above*) Numerous warehouses and vaults encouraged commercial enterprise.
119. (*opposite, below*) The *La Plata,* an unlucky ship that suffered particularly badly during the yellow fever season in the West Indies.

120 (*above*) The great steam companies required considerable space in the docks, and in 1851 the Inner Dock was completed.
121. (*below*) The Sailors' Home in Canute Road was established in 1861 to fulfil 'a constantly recurring need'.

122. 'Bustle and activity prevail on all sides; ships loading and unloading on the quays; steamships, and vessels c[...]
sizes, arriving and departing; waggons, carts and trucks, perambulating the streets; crowds arriving and departing[...]
at the Pier and Railway Stations; omnibuses and carriages of all sorts rattling through the streets; all tend to pro[...]
that the popular watering place has become an important commercial city. And what has been the magic agency[...]
achieve such a great good for the town? Steam both by land and sea, the Railroads and the Packets.' (Anon., 18[...]

123. Mid-Victorian Southampton, and the age of commerce dominated the horizon.

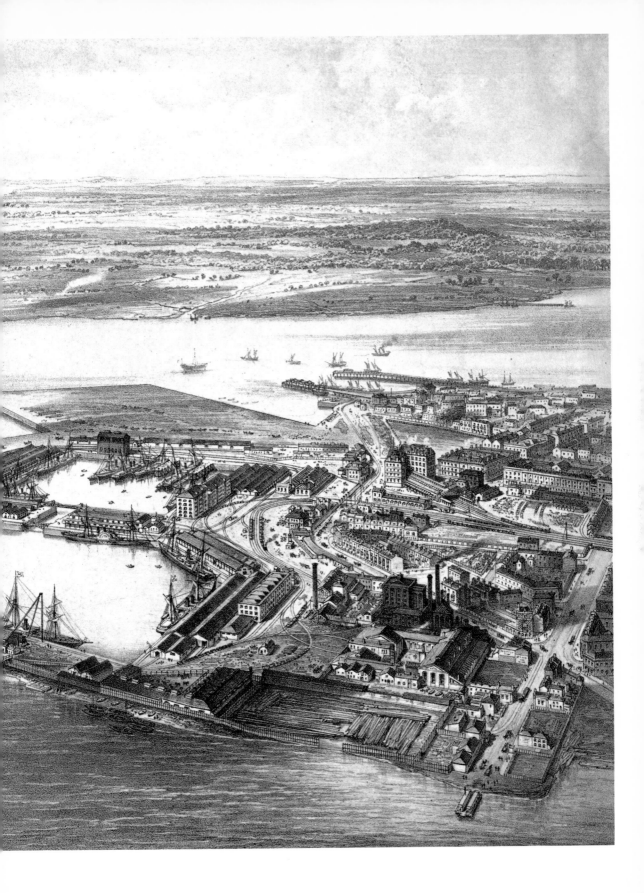